G000111938

The Five Mile Press Pty Ltd
1 Centre Rd, Scoresby
Victoria 3179 Australia
Email: publishing@fivemile.com.au
Website: www.fivemile.com.au

ISBN 978 1 74178 997 3

First published 2008

Printed in China 5 4 3 2 1

I just love that bag

ROBYN JOHNSON

ijustlovethat.net

As responsible publishers we feel that we should warn you that this book may lead you to increased thoughts of desire regarding bags along the lines of: "I've gotta have it or I'll die!"

Pleated satin evening bag with strass details. Dior, *c. 2007*.

Indispensables.

When fashions changed
around 1800, women no longer
wore costumes with full skirts
that concealed pockets. Instead,
they wore long, narrow, diaphanous
neoclassical styles. The need for a purse became obvious.
In England, these early accessories were called 'indispensables'
as they contained all the things a lady simply couldn't do without.

Velvet reticule embroidered with pearls and turquoise.
France, *c. 1850–70*.

Indispensable.

For around 200 years, women have been loath to dispense of this useful and wonderful accessory that has changed constantly to reflect their lives, independence and status.

Have women become so independent nowadays that they need oversized bags to carry all their indispensables? It depends …

Soft lambskin bowler with knotted fringe. Katherine Kwei, *c. 2008.*

Velvet handbag with gold-coloured frame and chain. Emilio Pucci, *c. 1960s.*

Linen and leather 'Love Birds' handbag. Enid Collins, *c. 1965.*

Mesh handbag with vanity case. Whiting & Davis, *c. 1920s.*

6

> *"The idea of seeing everybody clad the same is not really my cup of tea."*
> CHRISTIAN LACROIX

Silk Japanese kimono and leather handbag with lacquered wooden handles. Donna Webster, Kimono Collections, *c. 2007.*

Leaf motif handbag carried by Madonna at a premiere for the film *Evita*. Gianni Versace Couture, *c. 1997.*

> *"Fashion is not frivolous.*
> *It is part of being alive today."*

MARY QUANT

*I*n the 1920s, the wristlet came into vogue for two good reasons: it was no longer taboo for women to apply powder and lipstick in public, and flappers wanted their hands free for dancing. Modern designers like Timmy Woods and Lulu Guinness make bags that celebrate freedom, individuality and femininity with an added twist.

Beaded wristlet with plastic frame and beaded handle. France, *c. 1920s.*

8

Eiffel Tower bag with approximately 6,300 Swarovski crystals as carried by 'Carrie Bradshaw' in the film *Sex and the City*. Timmy Woods, *c. 2007*.

Novel birdcage wristlet. Lulu Guinness, *c. 2007*.

Plastic vanity case with lipstick in silk tassel. France, *c. 1925*.

"It is the unseen, unforgettable, ultimate accessory of fashion that heralds your arrival & prolongs your departure."

COCO CHANEL

Glossy 'broken glass' clutch. Nine West, *c. 2007.*

Fleur-de-lis leather handbag. Debbie Brooks, *c. 2007.*

Plasstic handbag with
strass decoration.
USA, *c. 1950s.*

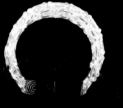

Crocheted handbag
with perspex handles.
France, *c. 1940s.*

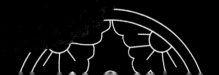

Origami-like
sculptural black
lucite box bag.
c. Unknown.

Leather vanity bag with metal frame
Elizabeth Arden, *c. 1965*

A portable dressing table.

A high-maintenance look requires constant touch ups—such pressure for an active girl. Solution, take everything you need in a vanity bag (not just a smaller make-up bag within a larger handbag) and go for a completely decked-out ordeal. Since their inception in the 1930s, these bags also came with a tiny light inside—just like a … you guessed it!

"Like a tabernacle, it's where women put the sacraments to make their beauty more so."

FRANÇOIS LESAGE

No more rummaging around. Black leather handbag featuring handy labelled compartments outside. Lulu Guinness, *c. 2007.*

"Fashions fade, style is eternal."
YVES SAINT LAURENT

*I*f you choose to invest in a bag made with beautiful workmanship, you want to be able to live with it for a lifetime. It is worth doing your research on bag design to ultimately choose a bag that fits with your own personal style and helps to define who you are.

Classic style with a sense of humour. Black leather handbag with pearlescent white lucite frame created to look like a set of teeth, with red leather interior—of course! Koro, *c. Unknown.*

"My mother and her mother, both of whom carried their whole lives in a handbag, were always prepared for anything." ANONYMOUS

Christian Dior's 1954 *The Little Dictionary of Fashion* advises: "Always the simplest and most classic handbags are the best and the quality of leather is very important."

Leather handbag with chrome ring as closure. Zumpole, *c. 1950s.*

Both the seen and unseen aspects of a woman's handbag say so much about her. On the outside is the public persona and often jammed inside is her private world.

16

sewing kit

Swiss Army knife

perfume

whistle

"*A woman's mind is as complex as the contents of her handbag; even when you get to the bottom of it, there is ALWAYS something at the bottom to surprise you!*"

socks

Band-Aids

photos

bottle of water

BILLY CONNOLLY

to-do list

tape measure

Classic Kelly

*O*riginally designed in 1935, the
Hermès bag that Grace Kelly carried
when she appeared in *Life* magazine
was renamed after her in 1956.
A single craftsman, hand-stitched
double saddle-stitch and 18 hours of
labour are the basis of each Kelly bag.

You carry a bag as a badge of who you are.

If your alligator should
retire in the evening,
what about your snake?

Aubergine alligator clutch, *c. 1930s.*

Snakeskin handbag. Kotur, *c. 2007.*

> *"The golden rule is that there are no golden rules."*
>
> GEORGE BERNARD SHAW

*I*f one were lucky enough to possess such charming creatures, would taking them out in the evening really be so wrong? The choice now belongs to the individual and sometimes the most impact comes from the unexpected.

Natural python bag with tortoise-shell finish jewellery. Dior, *c. 2007*.

21

*"Elegance does not consist
in putting on a new dress."*

COCO CHANEI

*I*ronically, what used to be conservative and appropriate
would be considered quite a statement today.

The 'rules' of appropriate dress—including 'How to
wear accessories'—were well defined up until the
changes in cultural freedom in the Sixties. Since then,
formality hasn't had a stronghold on fashion.

When was the last time that you bought matching
accessory ensembles? One has to admit that they make
quite an impact, probably even more so today.

23

You will never have to squeeze into your favourite handbag.

$\mathcal{D}$o all women suffer at some time from the 'Marie Antoinette Syndrome'? Are we all hopelessly attracted to new, gorgeous and extravagant items of beauty? Does it show by the way we stand in awe as we stare into shop windows, or how an item of fashion can catch our eye in the way that a bowerbird hones glittering prizes for its nest?

Some women will wear a handbag to define who they are, but is this just a foil for the true content of what's inside? Are all designer handbags just 'smoke and mirrors' or are some worth their weight in gold?

"When it comes to bags, men and cities, is it really what's outside that counts?"
CARRIE BRADSHAW, *SEX AND THE CITY*

Sensory overload.

('New bag' seduction–resistance is futile.)

SIGHT:
Beauty is in the eye of the beholder.

SMELL:
The smell of money. ('Exotic leather!')

'Lady Dior' bag in silver metallic lambskin. The 'Lady Dior' bag was presented to Diana, Princess of Wales, when it was launched in 1995. Dior, *c. 2007.*

TOUCH:
You touch my desire.

SOUND:
Tinkling charms.

TASTE:
A taste for designer luxury.

A life support system.

Ever had that terrible feeling of losing one's handbag? It's practically irreplaceable! No insurance policy would be able to cover its true value, especially when it is full of 'everything but the kitchen sink'.

French designers Jamin Puech have created gloriously individual handbags since 1990. Their bags are a unique blend of ideas, materials, craftspeople and manufacturers sourced from around the globe, free from the constraints of traditional leather manufacturing and uniform production.

Distinctive embellishment worth holding on to, **orange shoulder bag with chain straps.** Jamin Puech, *c. 2007.*

"A woman carries her neuroses in her handbag."
NATHALIE HAMBRO

29

To have and to hold.

*T*he clutch was introduced in 1916. It is always a great accessory to play with, quite literally. Whether you hold it or tuck it under your arm, the clutch is a fabulous piece for added attitude.

Patent metallic lambskin clutch featuring knot-inspired weave. Katherine Kwei, *c. 2008.*

> *"Elegance is refusal."*
> DIANA VREELAND

Metallic
snakeskin
clutch. Kotur,
c. 2008.

"I find that it is vital to have at least one type of handbag for each of the ten types of social occasion

MISS PIGG

1. Satin evening bag. Devi Kroell, *c. 2007.*
2. Embroidered bag. Dior, *c. 2007.*
3. Vintage patchwork needlepoint bag, *c. Unknown.*
4. Zebra clutch. Jimmy Choo, *c. 2007.*
5. Vintage anteater skin bag. French, *c. Unknown.*
6. Leather arm bag, *c. 1920s.*
7. Cherry bag with bow. Belinda O'Dea, *c. 2007.*
8. Velour tote. Kotur, *c. 2008.*
9. 'Lace fan' evening bag. Spencer & Rutherford, *c. 2008.*
10. Red lips clutch. Lulu Guinness, *c. 2007.*

2.

"Not So Formal"

1.

"Very Formal"

3.

"Just a Teensy Bit Formal"

4.

"Informal But Not That Informal"

"Every Day"

5.

"Every Other Day"

6.

9.

"Theatre"

7.

"Day Travel"

10.

8.

"Night Travel"

"Fling"

33

Status dressing without investing

Collage inspired by three great iconic bags. From left to right: Oh Chanel, you brilliant woman! Only you could have designed the 2.55 back in 1955. Another Hermès classic, this time named after Jane Birkin who shared a flight with an Hermès chairman and obviously made an impression with her need for a great bag to 'stow it all' in. And the forever sumptuous and sexy Fendi Baguette, almost good enough to eat.

in a whole wardrobe.

"When in doubt, overdress."

VIVIENNE WESTWOOD

Bag designer Lulu Guinness suggests, "Dress to suit your mood, don't keep your most glamorous things for special occasions." Agreed! Yet there is also the joy of the 'Cinderella transformation' when you change from the everyday and wear precious things that have been kept just for special.

Mesh handbag designed by Elsa Schiaparelli. Whiting & Davis, c. 1936–37.

Mesh shoulder bag with flap. Nine West, c. 2007.

Compact chain bag. Devi Kroell, c. 2007.

Satin clutch embroidered with strass. Dior, c. 2007.

I want it now! But I'll wait.

*D*esigner handbags now often outsell the clothes they share the catwalks with. So does the recent trend for oversized accessories reflect how important they have become? Add celebrity endorsement to this growing obsession and you may find the waiting list to obtain your 'it' bag too much to handle. So how about hiring a designer bag? Yes, that's right, and at least if you have to wait it may only be for a month as opposed to two years.

Red Hobo. Jimmy Choo, *c. 2007*.
Magenta bag, green bag. Dior, *c. 2007*.

"Attitude is everything." DIANE VON FÜRSTENBERG

*I*n the 1930s, Elsa Schiaparelli paved the way for surrealist concepts to be presented in fashion. Her Newsprint bag of 1934 (which looked like a folded newspaper) is just a simple example of her originality. Since then, many designers have been inspired by Ms. Schiaparelli's avant-garde approach.

Recycled book bag. Doublebooked Designs, *c. 2007.*

Bunch of roses bag. Lulu Guinness, *c. 2001.*

"A bag doesn't have to fit, and a bag doesn't have to be comfortable." LULU GUINNESS

A Deco-inspired clutch bag featuring a cat on the front and a mouse on the back. Luisa Clare, *c. 2007–08.*

1960s vintage brocade fabric clutch. Kotur, *c. 2007*.

Satin clutch with tassel. Jimmy Choo, *c. 2007*.

Silk evening bag with strass decoration and perspex frame. Maison de Bonneterie, *c. 1930s*.

"Be a caterpillar by day and a butterfly by night."
COCO CHANEL

Bejewelled velvet bag. Mary Frances, c. 2007.

Feathered bag with gold frame. Kotur, c. 2007.

Silk handbag woven in the Japanese Saga-Nishiki technique. The Netherlands, c. 1968–71.

"Personality begins when comparison ends."
KARL LAGERFELD

Opposite: 'Night' paper, feather and ribbon collage. Above: 'Day' ribbon and paper collage.

Photographic images kindly supplied by the following designers and establishments:

Belinda O'Dea: 33 (no.7).

Debbie Brooks: 10 (right).

Devi Kroell: 32 (no.1), 37 (left).

Dior: 3, 21, 27, 32 (no.2), 37 (right), 39 (both right).

Doublebooked Designs: 40 (right).

Getty Images: 12, 16, 28.

Jacqui Henshaw: photography of all collages.

Jamin Puech: 29.

Jimmy Choo: 32 (no.4), 39 (left), 42 (left).

Katherine Kwei: 5, 30.

Kimono Collections: 7 (right).

Kotur: 20 (left), 31, 33 (no.8), 42 (right), 43 (right).

Luisa Clare: 41 (both).

Lulu Guinness: 9 (centre), 13, 33 (no.10), 40 (left).

Mary Frances: 43 (centre).

Modbag (www.modbag.com): 11 (right), 14, 32 (no.3), 33 (no.5).

Museum of Bags and Purses, Herengracht 573, 1017 CD Amsterdam, The Netherlands (www.museumofbagsandpurses): 4, 6 (all), 7 (left), 8, 9 (right), 11 (left and centre), 12 (right), 15, 36 (left), 42 (centre), 43 (left).

Nine West: 10 (left), 36 (right).

Posh Girl Vintage Clothing (www.poshgirlvintage.com): 20 (right), 33 (no.6).

Spencer and Rutherford: 33 (no.9).

Timmy Woods: 9 (left).

For more information regarding The Museum of Bags and Purses: S. Ivo, *Bags*, Hendrikje: The Museum of Bags and Purses, Amsterdam, (The Pepin Press), 2004.

Please note: The author and publisher have made every effort to accurately cite the source or designer of each photographic image.

Also available in this exquisitely
packaged accessories trio:

'I just love that shoe'
'I just love that hat'

10 themed gift cards with envelopes
accompany each 48-page book.

ROBYN JOHNSON

Do you want more?

ijustlovethat.net

A website with links to designers,
museums and vintage sellers
and with information on where to buy
'I just love that...'
publications and stationery.